Magnetic Leadership

David —

Thanks for leading!

Vic Browning

Magnetic Leadership

Are you a good enough leader to be hired by the best employees?

by
Victor Downing

Global Advantage, Inc.
Palo Alto, California, U.S.A.
2005

Global Advantage, Inc.
510 Addison Ave.
Palo Alto, CA 94301
www.globaladvantageinc.net
Toll Free Number: 1-888-LEVELPL(AYING FIELD)
(1-888-538-3575)

First Printing

Printed in the United States of America

Library of Congress Control Number: 2005933246
ISBN-13: 978-0-9773138-0-8
ISBN-10: 0-9773138-0-8

Designed by Albert K. Lee

♻ Printed by a certified green printer with soy-based ink on recycled paper that is 100% post-consumer waste. This paper was also processed chlorine-free.

Contents

There Has Never Been A Greater Need For Leaders

For the first time in the history of work, what's best for the individual is best for business.

From the first day Adam weeded the garden, successful work amounted to people doing what they had to do faster, cheaper, and more attractively than their competitors. As a result, employees became headcount, labor units, full time equivalents... cordwood burned in the great corporate kiln.

Work has changed. Work is no longer simply, "Do what you're told to do." Work is, "Do what only you can do." Work has changed because what customers buy has changed. Today's customers no longer buy shoes, food, PCs, or haircuts. Today's customers buy speed, novelty, convenience, reliability, and entertainment that comes packaged as shoes, food, PCs, and haircuts.

These new customer requirements have created a demand for employees who are personable, resilient, ingenious, enthusiastic, healthy, and loyal[1]. Resilience, ingenuity, enthusiasm, et cetera cannot be bought. Such things must be volunteered. Such things are *discretionary*.

1

Leaders who expect to win in the new world of global work and who rely on "carrots" or "sticks" or both will fail. Successful leaders will be those individuals who *personally* attract people who are already *eager* to exceed account-abilities. Like championship athletes, great artists, and elite military personnel, these exceptional people are in search of the opportunity to do great work, to be the best in the world at something, to win and not just compete.

Are you a good enough leader to be "hired" by the best employees? Are you a *Magnetic Leader*?

---

[1] Before the abomination of September 11, 2001, many assumed such customer requirements (i.e., speed, novelty, convenience, etc.) were indulgences of a super-affluent society. The Post-September 11 world reveals that such requirements are all the more highly prized by customers. More than ever, customers want reliability, comfort, ease, predictability, convenience, etc. The only difference is that today customers also want to keep costs to a minimum. The challenge is tougher!

What Is A *Magnetic Leader?*

Magnetic Leaders have an uncanny ability to attract people who want to be part of a team that does more than get the job done.

Wages and benefits need to be competitive to be in the running for high-performance people, but economics is not the driving force for people who perform at an exceptional level... in fact, high-performance people will sometimes take a cut in pay for the opportunity to work on a team led by a *Magnetic Leader*. *Magnetic Leaders* have long since come to grips with the obvious: "If the basis for my relationship with the members of my team is economic, and if the members of my team are smart, then the members of my team will do everything they can to ensure that they give me *less* than I give them, and I will do the same thing. In the end, the members of my team become competitors for my resources, not assets in my quest for great achievements. The basis for exceptional work has got to be something more than money!"

Initiative, Guts, And Trust Are Worth More Than Money: *Magnetic Leaders* do not talk about new and more effective ways of leading; they actually lead in new and more effective ways. They

3

do not wait for a corporate initiative. They lead today, with today's budget and in today's political jungle. They do not lead with bravado, personal charisma, and catchy slogans; instead, they earn the dedication of the most astute and secure employees by committing their teams to extraordinary objectives and then entrusting the outcome to people who live to do more than money can buy.

Dignity, Candor, And Creativity Are Worth More Than Money: *Magnetic Leaders* lead to the peaks of profitability and quality. But *Magnetic Leaders* do more than that: they personally demonstrate how work itself is dignified and creative and that work is but one part of the best one has to give. These leaders work in ways that are creative and personable. These leaders have lives apart from work that are attractive and kind. These leaders tell the truth, don't "spin" bad news, and do everything possible to help members of the team achieve what is most personally prized even if it means losing a star performer. These leaders do whatever is required to ensure that all members of the team have every opportunity and encouragement to work in the same ways.

Self-Assessment
Are You A *Magnetic Leader?*

❑ Most members of your team exceed their accountabilities even though those accountabilities are extremely challenging.

❑ There is an unofficial waiting list to get on
your team.

❑ Members of your team *initiate* their performance reviews.

❑ Your meetings start on time, finish the agen-
da, and stop on time.

❑ Your team shows up with their To-Do's done.

❑ Members of your team confront each other—and you—when others drop the ball or
don't follow through.

❑ Members of your team challenge your "bright
ideas," sometimes making them brighter and
at other times saving you from yourself.

❑ It's not unusual for members of your team

to *initiate* discussions of career moves with you, even when those moves mean leaving your team.

❏ Other leaders routinely try to recruit members from your team.

❏ When you're out sick or on vacation, you don't have one eye on the job.

Who Are Those People You're Trying To Lead?

You lead a group of individuals: no two are alike and each functions best when he or she is engaged in personable, dignified, and unique ways. It is also true that each of these unique persons is one of three types: Polite Facade, Teetering, or Personal Best.

These types are not identified by their education, ethnicity, or tenure with the company. It's rare when they talk substantively about themselves and their work. When they do "speak," they often do so without using words.

Polite Facade: A few on your team appear to be allies but are actually *polite* saboteurs.

Lead this person by making certain that you and he or she has—and has documented—exactly the same understanding of what you expect and everything needed to succeed...*before* you begin. After you've done that, your job is to increase accountability and the frequency of reporting results. If you don't get results, document it, reset the goals, increase the frequency of reporting, and document some more. If results don't improve, "weed the garden."

Here's what people of the polite facade are "saying" to you:

- I look like I'm on your team, but actually I am just trying to stay off your radar.

- Without a literal display of our targets, I will continue to plead ignorance and argue that I have innocently misunderstood.

- Specific accountabilities are my worst enemy. They turn on the lights, eliminate excuses, and remove wiggle room. If you make my accountabilities specific and personal, I will do my best to obscure your expectations. If this fails, I'll try to build an alliance to oppose you. If this fails, I'll leave.

- I love long meetings where there's lots of talk but no conclusions are drawn. These meetings protect the status quo, give me insights on which way the wind is going to blow, and give me a breather from my work.

- If I can set the standards low enough I can live a fulfilled life.

- Why not leave well-enough alone?

- My work is different. It's complex and re-
  lationship-dependent. There are too many
  variables and too much judgment involved
  to reduce it to a diagramed flow chart. It
  might be a better use of the firm's funds to
  start in another part of the company.

- All these attempts at feedback, evaluation,
  ranking, et cetera, are worse than a waste
  of time. First of all they are purely subjec-
  tive, and secondly they undermine trust
  and teamwork in the organization.

- We need more accenting of the positive
  and less attention to what you don't like.
  After all, we've done it this way for a long
  time and done quite well, thank you very
  much. In the end your criticisms are really
  a matter of your style versus our style.

Teetering: Most of the people on your team tee-
ter between doing their personal best and a polite facade. This is the mother lode you want to
mine.

People in the Teetering category are con-
stantly assessing what is done—more than what
is said—that confirms what is most important to

you. You can lead these people by "setting them up for success," loudly "applauding" them when they succeed, making heroes out of those individuals and teams that perform at exceptional levels, and (possibly most importantly) by "weeding the garden."

Here is what people in the Teertering category are "saying" to you:

- What's the target? I hear the words about the way the leaders want us to work, but I see that those who get plum assignments operate in a completely different way.

- The leader for whom I'm willing to do exceptional work is one who: (1) works in a way I admire, (2) knows what I value most, (3), knows what stands in the way of what I value most, and (4) helps me isolate how this work will achieve or protect what I value most.

- If I'm going to stick my neck out, I need to *know* you're covering my back.

- When the future looks fuzzy to me, I hold a little back just in case things don't work out. I hold back some of my best ideas (they may help me make my next career move), I hold back some of my most penetrating criticisms (the powers that be may remember the pain I've caused when staffing decisions need to be made), and I hold back a little time (which I invest in networking and upgrading my resume). To put it plainly, the more ambiguity I face the less discretionary effort I deliver.

• When ambiguity hits our group I retreat to one of two caves. One of my caves is The Illusion Of Invulnerability. This is where I immerse myself in the fantasy that everything is OK, this too will pass, and positive attitudes get positive results. I know that if I just keep my head down and keep smiling, everything will be fine. My other cave is Fixation On The Fearsome. Behind an expression of dutiful attentiveness is a small army of ain't-it-awful evangelists who are preaching how bad it's going to be, why it's not fixable, and what I can do to stay off your radar screen long enough to find a safer place.

• I won't give you courageous and thoughtful feedback if you *can* make your numbers *apart* from my best efforts. I won't give you my most creative thinking if you can make your boss happy by delivering another version of the same old thing. If my career is advanced by misrepresenting others and kissing-up to you, I won't cut my teammates any slack or look out for their well-being. Likewise, I will not deliver discretionary effort if *you* do not deliver discretionary effort. This is simple: I will do what you do (not what you say) and I will do what we measure, not what we aspire to. I cannot give my full capacity to an effort that is vague. I need to know with certainty what we are going to achieve and how we will measure progress toward that achievement.

• The work I do determines the tools I bring to work. Ordinary work, ordinary tools. Extraordinary work: extraordinary tools. What work do you want me to do?

• Any goal-in-general is *not* my goal. A goal with my name on it is my goal.

• Let me save you alot of trouble: sending an e-mail, making a Power Point presentation, or funding an off-site will not communicate to me. What communicates to me is you: face-to-face, mid-stride, with backyard barbecue language.

Personal Best: A small number of your people are going to do their personal best *regardless* of your leadership. Take care of them because they are the people you are most likely to lose. The wonderful and scary truth is these people will perform at extraordinary levels with or without your leadership. When it becomes too much of a hassle to perform at high levels on your team, they will "fire" you and find a better leader.

Lead these people by serving these people. Give them a target. Give them what they need to succeed. Get out of the way. When they succeed—and they *will* succeed—"applaud" them in the ways they value most (and make sure your Teetering people know that the people in this category are your A-Team).

Here's what people in the Personal Best category are "saying" to you:

- If this is a place where "good-enough" is good enough, then this place is not good enough for me.

- I am eager to deliver truly exceptional work, but I will cease to do so if average team members benefit as much as those who do far more than they are paid to do.

- I'm not willing to sell my soul to the company store, but I am eager to give you a quality and volume of work you have rarely seen... if what I value most prospers in the process. I'm loaded with genius, creativity, enthusiasm, confidence, loyalty, courage, health, and many more assets that are not required by my job description. I'm grateful for the job but that's not enough. I need to make things happen. Truth be told, I don't want to compete... I want to win professionally and personally.

- If you don't, or can't, give me the tools, perspectives, and authority that are prerequisites to discretionary effort, then I can't and won't give you discretionary effort. Likewise, if my way-more-than-you-paid-for work is rewarded more or less like average work is rewarded, you will soon be seeing the last of me.

- The only way you're going to see me perform at maximum capacity is if you give me the authority I need to accomplish my accountabilities... and if you expect me to perform at high levels from the get-go, give me this authority up front and not in dribs and drabs as crises develop.

- I want to know where we are relative to where we said we'd be... and I want to know that frequently. I want to be on a team that is—as validated by data—the best at what we do (or at least way better than we were last year). I want to be back-to-back with other people who do not flinch under the bright lights of account-ability. I want to be led by someone who thrives on proven, superior performance. I want to win!

- I don't mind working hard, but I deeply resent working hard if that's what we do instead of working intelligently. If you don't have a grip on your processes, all you're left with is stupid, hard work.

Ambiguity Is Your Enemy

A fuzzy future, not-knowing, and ambiguity make people sick, make employees hedge their bets, turn leaders into mediocre managers, and destroy discretionary effort.

In World War II, the Nazis bombed London regularly, virtually the same time of day every week. In contrast, the suburbs of London were bombed infrequently and irregularly. The people of the suburbs had a much higher incidence of peptic ulcers per capita than did the citizens of London because the people in the city knew what was going to happen and the suburbanites did not. The message is clear: it's not bad news nor change that derails us. It's ambiguity.

Now consider the world of work. Success in business requires that you and your team continuously improve, reorganize, downsize, merge, upgrade, consolidate, retool, centralize, decentralize, divest, and acquire. Success generates ambiguity. The failure to continuously improve, reorganize, downsize, merge, upgrade, consolidate, retool, centralize, decentralize, divest, and acquire results in failure. Failure generates ambiguity.

When the future looks fuzzy most people on your team (including you) hold back. You hold

17

back information, your best ideas, and your most penetrating criticisms because you're not sure they are "solid" and you're afraid they will disturb the people on your team.

You can see where this is going: When the future is fuzzy, you hold back... and your team holds back. Everything starts winding down at exactly the time everything needs to ramp up.

The deck is stacked against you. Success generates new-hires, software upgrades, more alliances, and expanded accountabilities: success breeds ambiguity. Failure triggers layoffs, budget cuts, shifts in priorities, and less office space: failure breeds ambiguity. Competitors, regulators, economies, labor markets, terrorists, personal neuroses, corruption in the board room, and even the weather, all trigger change that transforms a beautifully functioning business plan into a snarled mass of confused, good intentions.

The environment breeds ambiguity. Ambiguity breeds restraint, hesitation... Ambiguity breeds ambiguity. Like a metastasizing cancer, prolonged ambiguity generates bad decisions, discouragement, and animosity. Discouragement and animosity proliferate more ambiguity and bad decisions.

What *Magnetic Leaders* Do

Magnetic *Leaders* burn off the ambiguity.

In the same way the real value of every great chef is an extraordinary dining experience[2] (rather than the provision of a safely prepared, nutritious plate of consumables), so too the value you bring is the provision of a sharply focused future (not just the provision of a reasonable and resourced plan).

You can burn off the ambiguity using five ancient principles:

1. Pursue What You Cannot Do.

2. Make The Invisible Visible.

3. Invest In The Best.

4. Weed The Garden.

5. Rest and Remember Regularly.

---

[2] Please see B. Joseph Pine II and James H. Gilmore, <u>The Experience Economy: Work is Theatre & Every Business a Stage</u>, (Boston: Massachusettes: Harvard Business School Press, 1999). This very brief and substantive book (more than any other) establishes the progression of work economies and the necessity of what I have called "discretionary effort" to succeed in the current and future economies.

Magnetic Leadership is what ordinary people have done throughout the ages to unearth extraordinary performance from other ordinary people, especially under adverse conditions. Patton and Gandhi, Mother Teresa and Christopher Columbus, Joshua and Sun Tzu, Sir Winston Churchill and powerful parents of every generation... all have been known by these five principles.

The best way to implement the five principles of *Magnetic Leadership* is in three steps:

Step One: Lay The Foundation

- *Pursue What You Cannot Do.*
- *Make The Invisible Visible.*

Step Two: Improve Performance

- *Invest In The Best.*
- *Weed The Garden.*

Step Three: Build Momentum

- *Rest and Remember Regularly.*

Starting with *Pursuing What You Cannot Do* makes sense because if you are attempting a goal that does not require discretionary effort, bother with leadership in the first place? Giving attention to *Making The Invisible Visible* is a prudent next step because if your people can't see where they're going, then you certainly can't make them accountable for getting there.

Investing in The Best and *Weeding The Garden* tend to happen simultaneously. There is, however a fair bit of judgment you need to apply here. If it's clear that you have entrenched Never-Evers on your team, or processes that just won't work no matter how hard you try, then weed the garden sooner rather than later. On the other hand, if the weeds are hard to distinguish at first, then invest in the best so that the differences become clear as quickly as possible.

Resting and Remembering Regularly is important because it is what your team *remembers*, not what your team has done, that determines what your team will do. This step needs to bring up the rear because you need to have an honorable track record before you invest time in considering it.

Principle # 1: *Pursue What You Cannot Do*

Why don't team members complain when meetings start late, members fail to do what they said they would do, and when office politics have more influence on decisions than data? Why do exceptional performers quietly leave such teams and take on the risks of a different team? What do teams that perform at exceptional levels have that most teams lack?

Unfortunately, most leaders want to finish more than they want to win. They set ordinary goals that are good enough to keep the lights on, but not much more. Second, most leaders can get their teams to do great things—in the short run—by compensating for substandard leadership with extraordinarily long work days.

Ordinary goals attract ordinary performance… and ordinary goals repel those who want to do great things. Who do you want on your team?

Short-term success at the expense of sleep and life-apart-from-work is titillating to naïve junior members with no obligations and burned-out veterans who need their next adrenalin fix, but that kind of leadership seems silly to those with a life and a backbone. Who do you want on your team?

Are you aiming too low? Are you pursuing goals that require too little, goals that can be achieved *apart from* the discretionary effort of your people? It may be that you need to attempt greater things at work... or it may be that you need to help your people attempt great things in their lives at work or apart from work. But in either case, if *you* don't attempt goals that are beyond your *personal* ability to achieve, you will never earn discretionary effort from your people.

Self-Assessment
Principle # 1: *Pursue What You Cannot Do*

Answer each of the following questions, "Yes," or, "No." Don't ride the fence.

For each item you answer, "Yes," ask yourself, "What physical evidence do I have that this answer is true?" Chances are if you lack physical evidence of your affirmative answer, you've done more in your mind than you've done in fact. If that's the case, change your answer to, "No."

For each item you answer, "No," pull out your calendar and commit yourself to specific actions on specific dates with specific people. (The questions themselves should point you in the direction of the action you should take.)

See chart next page

Yes	No	
		1. Have you won the commitment of your team to a business goal that would require their more-than-I'm-paid-for (i.e., discretionary) effort?
		2. Have you confirmed that each person on your team understands the specific kinds of discretionary effort you expect of each person the same way you understand those things?
		3. Does achievement of the team's goals give you what is most important to you and/or protect what you value most against what most threatens that?
		4. Do the people on your team know you—the real you—well enough that they would feel confident in sharing the same level of information about themselves?

Yes	No	
		5. Have you confirmed the ambitions and motivations of the people in your group? Have you confirmed with each member those things that threaten or impede what is valued most highly?
		6. Have you confirmed with each member how the delivery of discretionary effort at work will help each member of the team achieve what's most important to each member?
		7. Are you pursuing what is best for the people who are on your team?
		8. If today were your last day, would you have rich and robust and inspiring memories of your leadership and the members of your team and what you and your team did together?

Principle # 2: *Make The Invisible Visible*

(Part 1: What Do You Expect?)

In the same way a soccer coach must continuously convince players they can be a championship team *before* they win the championship, so too you must win the allegiance of each member of your team *before* they have achieved anything. They must *see* the potential to win—not just compete—and they must literally *see* what winning looks like.

There are four otherwise invisible essentials that each member of your team needs to see every day as clearly as you see the gauges on the dashboard of your car:

1. They each must *see* where you are taking them... the results or outcomes that will be achieved.

2. They each must see that they have sufficient "fuel in the tank" to go the distance. This includes: access to people and information, a command of the big picture, personal authority, clarity of accountabilities,

equipment, space, people, money, and the assurance of late-breaking information that might impact personal success.

3. They each must see the entire process by which they will take the "handoff" from those upstream in the value chain and give the "handoff" to those downstream in the value chain; furthermore, they each must see the "gauges" which tell them how well the process is performing *while it is underway*.

4. They each must see the specific, person-to-person behaviors that will be characteristic of a winning team.

In many ways, doing superior work is like taking a successful, cross-country trip. If your car has no fuel gauge, you will drive more slowly, stop more often for gas, and attempt shorter trips. When you help your people see where the team is going, they know what kinds of clothes to pack. Seeing the road that will be traveled tells the team what kind of vehicle to choose. Seeing where they have been tells the team what they are capable of.

Self-Assessment Principle # 2: *Make The Invisible Visible*

(Part 1: What Do You Expect?)

Answer each of the following questions, "Yes," or, "No." Don't ride the fence.

For each item you answer, "Yes," ask yourself, "What physical evidence do I have that this answer is true?" Chances are if you lack physical evidence of your affirmative answer, you've done more in your mind than you've done in fact. If that's the case, change your answer to, "No."

For each item you answer, "No," pull out your calendar and commit yourself to specific actions on specific dates with specific people. (The questions themselves should point you in the direction of the action you should take.)

See chart next page

Yes	No	
		1. Do you <u>visually</u> display what your team will accomplish, your team's intended outcomes? ("Visually display" does *not* mean posted on a website. "Visually display" means low-tech, on the wall in a semi-public place.)
		2. Have you discussed with each member of the team the resources available to him/her, the team's end-to-end process, specific accountabilities, authority, tools, training and other resources, et cetera?
		3. Do you <u>visually</u> display the six or fewer key behaviors without which your team will fail in its pursuit of extraordinary performance?
		4. Do you spend more time with your "stars" than with your "squeaky wheels"?

Yes	No	
		5. Do your people literally lay eyes on you *at least* once a month?

Principle # 2: *Make The Invisible Visible*

(Part 2: Inspect What You Expect)

Just as a basketball team won't win without reviewing game tapes, analyzing game stats, and then making adjustments in the next game, so too your team won't win without an ongoing, hardnosed examination of performance data.

You must evaluate the objective measures of what's most important to your team's success. These will be databased indicators like the following:

- the extent to which the team is achieving end-of-game/quarter-end/year-end performance goals.

- the extent to which you are giving the team what they need to succeed in achieving their accountabilities.

- the extent to which the work processes are consistently giving your customers what they want.

- the extent to which the members of the team are routinely doing the behaviors that are essential to the success of the team.

Although inspecting what is expected is essential to superior performance, it will be met with passive and active resistance. Not only that, successful inspection causes submerged problems to pop to the surface. At least for a time, productivity will suffer, morale will be threatened, and things will look worse. On the other hand, no team that performs at exceptional levels over a significant duration has done so without taking frequent, regular, courageous looks at the way things really are.

Self-Assessment Principle # 2: *Make The Invisible Visible*

(Part 2: Inspect What You Expect)

Answer each of the following questions, "Yes," or, "No." Don't ride the fence.

For each item you answer, "Yes," ask yourself, "What physical evidence do I have that this answer is true?" Chances are if you lack physical evidence of your affirmative answer, you've done more in your mind than you've done in fact. If that's the case, change your answer to, "No."

For each item you answer, "No," pull out your calendar and commit yourself to specific actions on specific dates with specific people. (The questions themselves should point you in the direction of the action you should take.)

See chart next page

Yes	No	
		1. Do the members of your team give you regular and frequent feedback on:
		a. The extent to which they understand how their team adds value to the business overall
		b. The extent to which they correctly understand the issues of greatest importance to your customers
		c. The degree to which each member knows his or her personal accountabilities
		d. The extent to which each member has sufficient decision-making authority to achieve his or her accountabilities

Yes	No	
		1. Do the members of your team give you regular and frequent feedback on:
		e. The extent to which each member has sufficient skill, equipment, space, and help from others
		f. The extent to which each member has sufficient access to information and persons
		g. The extent to which each member feels that his or her excellent work is seen and appreciated in ways that he or she values most

Yes	No	
		1. Do the members of your team give you regular and frequent feedback on:
		h. The extent to which each member is confident you will inform him or her of inbound changes soon enough to adjust and still achieve the accountability, or, if there is insufficient time to adjust, the extent to which each member is confident you will be fair in evaluating performance even though an accountability has not been achieved owing to changes beyond his or her control
		2. Do you and the members of your team regularly review the effectiveness of your entire work process?

Yes	No	
		3. Do you and the members of your team regularly review objective measures of the extent to which each member is interacting with the other members of the team in ways that will lead to exceptional performance?
		4. Do you and the members of your team regularly review the results or outcomes they have achieved?
		5. When the data show that your team is not performing according to standard (see above), do you discover and record the cause(s) in a systematic fashion, and then develop a written plan for getting back on track?

Principle # 3: *Invest in The Best*

"The things that grow are the things you feed."[3]

"Investing in The Best" is counterintuitive. Everything in you wants to "grease that squeaky wheel." Although you must attend to those "squeaky wheels," it is even more important that you do more of what is working well.

As a leader, you need to grow three crops: (1) business partners who give you more value than you have contracted for, (2) customers who help you beat the competition to the punch, and (3), team members who deliver discretionary effort.

Business partners grow when they are involved earlier and more substantially in your planning and problem-solving processes. Customers grow when they are invited to describe how you can better serve them. Team members grow when they are given the opportunity and the resources to do truly extraordinary, dignified, personally-valued work.

Obviously helping members of your team grow is a leadership accountability, but helping your customers and business partners grow may

---

[3] Roy Downing (my dad).

not seem like something a leader does. Whether obvious or not, the fact is that you will not achieve extraordinary results and you cannot develop your people if you do not help your business partners and customers.

The "food" may surprise you: time, authority, and influence. If you're not "feeding" your stars more than your problem children, your A-customers rather than your C-customers, your most trusted business partners than your gotta-watch-'em-close partners, then you are probably growing the wrong things.

Self-Assessment
Principle # 3: *Invest in The Best*

Answer each of the following questions, "Yes," or, "No." Don't ride the fence.

For each item you answer, "Yes," ask yourself, "What physical evidence do I have that this answer is true?" Chances are if you lack physical evidence of your affirmative answer, you've done more in your mind than you've done in fact. If that's the case, change your answer to, "No."

For each item you answer, "No," pull out your calendar and commit yourself to specific actions on specific dates with specific people. (The questions themselves should point you in the direction of the action you should take.)

See chart next page

Yes	No	
		1. Do you have written criteria for evaluating your internal/ external customers (i.e., those who are downstream from you)?
		2. Do you have written criteria for evaluating your business partners (i.e., those who are upstream from you)?
		3. Do you have objective measures for determining those members of your team who are best demonstrating the team's key behaviors?
		4. Do you give more of your time to your best performers than to those whose performance is mediocre or poor?
		5. Do you invest the time and money required to "map" your team's most important processes?

Yes	No	
		6. Do you invest the time and money required to collect process-related data on your team's most important processes?
		7. Do you invest the time and money required to use process-related data to improve the performance of your team's most important processes?
		8. Do you talk candidly to your team about what is most important from your perspective?
		9. Do you listen? When others speak, are you silent? Do you play back what others say in ways that cause them to confirm that you "got it"?
		10. Do you give your high-performance people more accountability, access to people and information, and rewards than you give to lesser-performing members of your team?

Principle #4: *Weed The Garden*

Leading is like gardening... if you don't pull out the weeds, you won't harvest the tomatoes.

"Weeds" come in many forms. "Weeds" are unpredictable and wasteful processes, rumors and gossip, and the people of the polite facade. The people of the polite facade say the right words but never deliver more than ordinary and substandard work... while skillfully pointing to the reasons that the best could not be done. In the extreme, the people of the polite facade are those who invisibly ignite insurrection, insubordination, and campaigns of no confidence.

"Weeding the garden"—without "pulling out the tomatoes"—sounds alot easier than it is. "Weeding" requires attention to detail, timing, and reliance on facts, not opinions. If you don't carefully monitor the time and money you spend improving processes, you'll blow your budget and miss your deadlines. "Weeding the garden" can result in lawsuits, accusations, and blacklisting. Confronting rumors and replacing them with truth may expose pockets of saboteurs who retaliate against the light. Turning on the lights on political games may be a noble thing to do, but if it isn't handled properly, it can be the last noble thing you do. "Weeding the garden" is an unpleasant activity for all concerned... and it is especially unpleasant for the leader.

In addition to being unpleasant, "weeding the garden" seems harsh and distrustful. You want to believe that time, positive expectations, and encouragement make bad things better. That's never the case in the garden, and it's rarely the case at work.

Most leaders wait too long to do the "weeding."

Self-Assessment
Principle # 4: *Weed The Garden*

Answer each of the following questions, "Yes," or, "No." Don't ride the fence.

For each item you answer, "Yes," ask yourself, "What physical evidence do I have that this answer is true?" Chances are if you lack physical evidence of your affirmative answer, you've done more in your mind than you've done in fact. If that's the case, change your answer to, "No."

For each item you answer, "No," pull out your calendar and commit yourself to specific actions on specific dates with specific people. (The questions themselves should point you in the direction of the action you should take.)

See chart next page

Yes	No	
		1. Do you have data—not just feelings—that tell you where each member of your team is relative to your team's key behaviors?
		2. Do you personally observe behavior or performance "weeds" before you start "weeding the garden"?
		3. Do you personally meet with members of the team who have behavior or performance "weeds" and confirm what is happening before you start taking action?
		4. Do you personally meet with members of the team who have behavior or performance "weeds" and write an action plan for removing those "weeds" and have them endorse that plan?

Yes	No	
		5. Do you meet with members of the team who have behavior or performance "weeds" at least one time after writing an action plan and before you initiate more drastic action?
		6. Do you consult with HR before terminating a person or making a significant change in his or her employment status?
		7. Do you have process indicator data (i.e., regularly collected data that reliably show how well your team's work processes are performing) that show you the presence of "process-weeds" or "process-tomatoes"?

Yes	No	
		8. Do you have process quality data (i.e., regularly collected data that reliably show the extent to which your team is giving your customers what they expect from your processes) that give you objective evidence of the extent to which your processes are satisfying your customers?
		9. Do you use a systematic, data-based process for finding process indicator and quality indicator deficiencies?
		10. When there is an important "change in the air," do you aggressively collect rumors from members of your team and replace those rumors with facts?

Principle # 5: *Rest and Remember Regularly*

The longer you are a leader, the more you know there are precious few things you can "make happen." The truth is you don't control much at all. You can't predict what will happen with markets, economies, politics, corporate strategies, or even with your well-conceived plan. It is even impossible to predict how much longer you will enjoy today's success or endure its difficulties. You can't predict how much longer your star performers will stay with you or how much longer you must endure the Teflon employees who add no value. Ambiguity is your environment.

It's even worse for your team. The same fog that surrounds you surrounds the members of your team, but they lack the radar you enjoy. They don't sit in the planning meetings that review data on market trends. They don't get an advanced peek at the budget that ensures or eliminates their spot on next year's team. They don't enjoy the confidence that comes from spending several hours with your colleagues who lead teams upon which your team depends. Unlike those on your team, you decide what you do by telling your people what they will do. There's more fog at the bottom of the organization chart than at the top.

If there is nothing your team can experience on a regular and frequent and *predictable* basis, then everything is (effectively) out of control... and that's very bad for business! The antidote to the fog of ambiguity is predictability, regularity, and the certainty that something specific will happen at a definite time.

It's important to stop work regularly and predictably... it's *not* important to stop work for a long time. Remember: the essential benefit is the knowledge that you—and therefore your team—are in control of the work... even to the point of stopping it. Fifteen minutes of no work in the middle of a workday can contribute as much—maybe more—to the team's sense of control as eight hours in a company barbecue on the weekend.

Long periods of success are energizing, but they are also exhausting because success without pause is like a drug addiction: it carries you until you crash. Resting is important *not*, in the first place, because your team is tired and needs a nap. The principal value of resting is the *predictable* experience of *not* working—even if only for a few moments. Resting converts work from something that possesses your people, to something over which you and your people have control. This is particularly valuable when everything is working well.

Remembering is important *not*, in the first place, because your team needs a pep rally or a history lesson. The principal value of remembering is the *predictable* experience of *not* working—even if for only a few moments. In addition, helping your team remember the triumphs and tragedies of their history can bring great confidence and humility to teams which are easily lost in the fog of today's pressing events.

If going to work becomes a constant blur of activities that start in the first quarter and end in the fourth quarter, then your people will—at best—make endurance and not ingenuity and enthusiasm the norm. Like a good movie, a great book, or a wonderful dinner party, high-performance teams have rhythm and variety. The rhythm of those teams is some version of: preview-work-rest-remember-preview. It is never work-work-work-work.

It is what your team *remembers*, not what your team has done, that determines what your team will do.

Self-Assessment
Principle # 5: *Rest and Remember Regularly*

Answer each of the following questions, "Yes," or, "No." Don't ride the fence.

For each item you answer, "Yes," ask yourself, "What physical evidence do I have that this answer is true?" Chances are if you lack physical evidence of your affirmative answer, you've done more in your mind than you've done in fact. If that's the case, change your answer to, "No."

For each item you answer, "No," pull out your calendar and commit yourself to specific actions on specific dates with specific people. (The questions themselves should point you in the direction of the action you should take.)

Yes	No	
		1. Do the members of your team spontaneously recount the victories, accomplishments, and heroes from the team's history?
		2. Is there a visible representation of the history of your team in a heavily trafficked area?
		3. Are the on-the-job accident rates of your people below the company/industry average?
		4. Are meetings on time, crisp, productive, and encouraging?
		5. Are the members of the team able to have a life apart from work without fear that at-home commitments may get broken by at-work emergencies?

Yes	No	
		6. Are the members of the team taking their vacation time?
		7. Are the sick days taken by members of the team within or below the norm?
		8. Do the members of the team look rested and confident?
		9. Are you rested and confident?
		10. Do the members of your team take a break—a real break—several times during the day?
		11. When tensions escalate, do the members of your team respond calmly and helpfully?
		12. Do you leave work at work when you go home?

Yes	No	
		13. Do the people on your team leave work at work when they go home?
		14. When faced with a tough problem, is it common for members of your team to reference examples from the history of the team?
		15. Is it common to hear a member of your team refer the team to past successes when you have to announce bad news?
		16. Does your team have traditions, slogans, icons, memorabilia, or unique sayings that they prize highly?

How Did You Get To Where You Are? Will You Choose To Go Farther?

More likely than not, you were pushed into leadership because you succeeded as an individual contributor. You may have hesitated, wondering if you should leave the safe harbor of predictable success; but soon you let go the bow and stern lines, and set sail for a bright horizon. In the early days you were thrilled by the certain knowledge that you could make things better... alot better. And, let's be honest, the fatter paycheck and special privileges of leadership were a whole lot better than the alternative.

Sooner or later you discovered the dirty underbelly of leadership.

Your boss required more of you... but didn't provide more resources. Your people smiled and nodded in agreement with the corporate plans you dutifully delivered to them... and continued to do the same work in the same way. You built trust and rapport with colleagues in management off-sites... and fell victim to well-honed political knives when it was time for budget review. It was not long until the people at home let you know you were not there enough, while the people at work resented you for having so many privileges while doing so little "real work."

It would be hard to "go back." No doubt you have elevated and expanded your lifestyle in proportion to the increase in pay. But, it's more than money that keeps you on the leadership track. You've helped the organization make great leaps forward... and you know you can do more. You've treasured the gratitude of those few who did more than they ever dreamed they could do... and they credited you with that. Although you rarely (if ever) talk about it, you feel largely responsible for the well being of those who work for you, as well as for the families they support... and you don't want to leave them in the lurch.

Like all leaders who actually lead (as opposed to simply sit behind the leader's desk), you face a daily dilemma. On the one hand your greatest satisfaction has resulted from the extraordinary goals you have set, the bold moves to which you have committed your team, and the risky assignments you have entrusted to your people. On the other hand it doesn't take much for people who are dug into the status quo to topple the efforts of those who aim high. Is it any wonder that you regularly calculate how you can make the career finish line by attempting lesser goals?

What Kind Of Leader Are You?

When business magazines and employees talk about great business leaders, they describe men (almost always it's men) who "make things happen," "inspire the troops," overcome obstacles, defeat the opponents, "pull us together," and above all else "succeed."

You aspire to that... and to more than that.

Leadership is more than unusual personal gifts that capture the imaginations of people and move them toward a common goal. Osama Ben Laden, Adolf Hitler, Joseph Stalin, Pol Pot, Fastow, and Kozlowski are men (almost always it's men) who, for a long time, "made things happen," "inspired the troops," overcame obstacles, defeated opponents, "pulled us together," and above all else "succeeded." These are not leaders. These are egotistical demigods who lived to be followed.

Leadership is not defined by a constellation of competencies. Leadership is defined by its consequences.

Leading is doing. Leading is not talking about doing. Leading is not getting other people to do things. Leading is doing. Leading is Gandhi taking the first blow, Mother Teresa bathing the leper, Joshua spying on the enemy, Churchill opposing Parliament, and Jesus on the cross. Leaders remove freeloaders, nay-sayers, and corruptors and invest their time in individuals who take smart risks, own failures, and who find new ways to benefit customers. Leaders do what they want to see others do: they show up on time with their work done, listen more than they speak, tell the truth, and don't gossip.

Leading is doing what's *right*. This is why Mother Teresa is a leader and Osma Ben Laden is a selfish coward. You know what's "right." It's the way you would be pleased to have your children treated. Leadership gives more than it takes and draws out that which is honorable in others. Truth, justice, mercy, redemption, courage, patience, kindness, humility, creativity, and beauty are right. Partial truth, prejudice, inflexibility, waste, cowardice, impatience, violence, arrogance, selfishness, and ugliness are not right.

Leading attracts wise people. The measure of a leader is not the number of the followers. The measure of the leader is the caliber of the followers. Are experienced, observant, capable people drawn to you, or are you followed by impressionable, naïve, and scheming people? Leaders attract high performers and draw out the best in most people... they are *magnetic*.

You may be extroverted, introverted, emotional, rational, social, misanthropic, male, female, educated, uneducated, old, young, experienced, inexperienced, liberal, or conservative. In every case, a leader draws the best out of people regardless of circumstances.

Leading is doing the right thing first such that wise people follow.

Are You A Leader Or A Manager?

What is it about leadership that attracts you? Are you attracted to leadership or are you repelled by the prospect of management?

Most people are attracted to an outsider's view of leadership. The term, "leadership," has the panache of "visionary," "strategist," "thinker," and "catalyst." Is your picture of a leader one who relates to the common worker like a benevolent lord relates to his serfs, is able to see beyond the horizon, and is the otherwise unavailable source of motivation, vision, insight, and inspiration? You may think—or hope—that tactics and pesky details are to leaders what a traffic jam is to an Indy-500 racecar. But in reality, those are the assumptions of pretenders who are enamored with their quasi-mystical "potential" but who accomplish nothing more than winning the adolescent admiration of the naïve and neurotic.

"I lead. Others manage." "My gift is leadership. I'm not gifted when it comes to the details." "I need someone to take care of those things, so I can lead." Such is the arrogance of egotists, demigods, and those who have never attempted anything truly great. In fact, leaders who are not excellent managers are like racecars without steering wheels or musicians who are late for the concert.

Great leaders, like great artists and great athletes, do the fundamentals exceptionally well all the time. Musicians practice their scales for hours every day, for every year of their career. World-class basketball players practice free throws, dribbling, and lay-ups. When it comes to businesses, organizations, and governments, the fundamentals are planning, staffing, organizing, and controlling... management.

If you are a leader, there is no route around planning. Your plans need to be replete with intelligence, performance indicators, and contingencies... and so well-developed that they appear to be simple. You will soon be "led" by your planners if you cannot quickly spot the bravado, conflict, or cowardice in a plan *by looking at the details*. Leaders know a good plan when they see it because leaders have developed good plans.

Why do exceptional people surround some leaders but not others? Do you really think those who have great teams are the beneficiaries of inspirational speakers with esoteric visions or HR departments with the inside track on recruiting? Not hardly! You will have a great team if you know how to *personally* spot, challenge, develop, support, and care for your people. It's called "staffing" and it's much more than "filling a slot" on an organization chart. Only a leader can put together a team that is the envy of the competition. Leaders, like musical composers, integrate the efforts of many individuals into a single voice. They organize. It is not enough for you to "give your people the vision." It is not enough for you to have a plan. Beyond that, the work of each person and each group must pass seamlessly to the next contributor in the process. You must be able to look at an organization chart, a floor plan, and a process map and quickly spot unnecessary steps, potential conflict, and opportunities to delight customers that are forfeited as a result of how things are organized.

If you are not interested in "the details," then you are like a ship's captain who is not interested in the latest weather report, the destination, the current position, or the rate of fuel consumption. Suicide! You need to be so "in-tune" with "the ship" that you sense an emerging problem by a "shift in the vibration of the deck beneath your feet." Although you may never "put your hands on the wheel" or "turn a wrench in the engine room," you have got to be in control of the "ship" *in detail.*

It's impossible for you to *personally* plan, staff, organize, and control anything much more complex than a birthday party. Your success depends on the ability of others to manage also. Your life is in their hands. How will you select those in whom you place so much trust? How will you know if they are doing what they should be doing? You cannot rely on your inspirational words, your captivating vision of the future, or your deep insights to provide that assurance. You've got to be a good enough manager to spot a bad one, and you must *personally* own the planning, staffing, organizing, and controlling of those who report to you directly.

Management is a part of leadership like the left bicycle pedal is part of the right bicycle pedal. You've got to have both.

Are You Sure You Want To Be A Leader?

Too often those who aspire to leadership do so with the fantasies of a follower rather than with the scars of a leader. In fact, leading has far less to do with the corner office, the stock options, and the inspirational speech than with attention to detail, preparation, and plain, hard work.

Leading is messy, like gardening, making pottery, and giving birth is messy. You're leading a group of people who are tired, dubious, preoccupied with at-home issues... and—most of them, at least—packed with the irrepressible drive to do something truly exceptional. Unfortunately, some members of your team are Never-Evers: they will never, ever do more than they are paid to do, never, ever challenge the status quo, and never, ever be motivated by anything more than getting more than they give.

You are expected to lead now. The clock is running, money is on the table, and there's blood on the floor. Your superiors may be short-sighted, petty, and incompetent. More likely than not, your budget is inadequate, the training is insufficient, and the competition is gaining on you. Nevertheless, you will lead or you will settle for what comes your way.

Leadership success is not a function of doing the right thing. Successful leadership is a function of doing the right thing such that most of your people do the right thing. But not everyone wants to do the right thing. Many will respond to the clear light of accountability like vampires respond to the rising sun. Therefore doing the right thing by getting rid of some people is likely to force those who want to freeload and detract to get with the program or find another place to work.

Anyone who knows anything about leadership doesn't want to be one. Yes, it's better to fly Business Class than coach and better to have an office with a door than to work in a cubicle, but it's tough to trust so much to so many and to know that your poor decisions can cause great distress for more people than you will know. It's tough to present your people with a future full of hope and opportunity and then to chaff against other leaders who are shortsighted, incompetent, and dishonest. Leadership is expensive.

Why lead?

You've got a target in sight that is more compelling than the expense and the risk of leadership. That target may be sharply focused or barely discernable, but it's there. There's only one way to hit that target: you've got to lead a team that routinely does more than they are paid to do. You need people who are attracted to a goal that is unachievable apart from genius, creativity, enthusiasm, courage... *discretionary effort.* You must become a magnet to people like that.

Are You Responsible For Everything?

Yes.

The success of an enterprise rests most heavily on the shoulders of its leaders. Leaders make the *first* move in the right direction in ways that wise people follow. Leaders—not those who follow them—are responsible for providing the conditions within which others can do their best work... but that is *not* the whole picture.

Not every employee *wants* to deliver a fair day's work for a fair day's pay... and much less do they want to deliver discretionary effort. A person in this category keeps a very close tally on what-I'm-paid-to-do versus what-I-am-doing; if the latter exceeds the former, these people feel "ripped-off," exploited, and defeated in their quest to "get a better deal" from work.

That point of view may be understandable. Some have been "ripped-off" or exploited (at work or elsewhere) and have vowed that they would never again suffer that indignity. Or, they may have no experience working for a *Magnetic Leader* and have concluded that those who appeal to employees for discretionary effort are either naïve or con artists. On the other hand, some may simply be more dedicated to getting the greatest monetary return for their hourly investment than they are attracted to excellence, achievement, learning, and esprit de corps. In any case, if you have done due diligence to address the concerns of these people and they do only what they are paid to do, then it is your responsibility to move them out of your team or into work that requires no discretionary effort.

Likewise, not everyone is *capable* of delivering discretionary effort. Some have a life apart from work that is so demanding that going to work is restful by comparison. Others have intellectual or physical limitations that make the kinds of discretionary effort you need truly beyond their grasp. Again, the job of a *Magnetic Leader* is to move these people out of your team or into work that requires no discretionary effort.

A rare few—not more than 5%—deliver discretionary effort regardless, or in spite of, their leaders. They are indomitable in their pursuit of a better way, a stronger team, and a higher goal. They are new world migrant workers, incessantly in search of a bigger canvas to paint, a higher mountain to climb, a more difficult problem to solve. They know what they need to succeed and they go out and get it. They manage their at-home lives well and keep their lives balanced overall, and become more composed and confident as the pressure rises. Your challenge with these people is to give them the opportunity to do their best work and then get out of the way.

Most employees, however, are diamonds-in-the-rough when it comes to discretionary effort. It makes sense that you have more diamonds-in-the-rough than you have diamonds. Until very recently, discretionary effort has been essential only in crises, calamities, and start-ups. Most people have no role model for a person who delivers discretionary effort, no tenure with a *Magnetic Leader*, no experience with the thrill of doing-more-than-I-ever-thought-I-could-do. Given the opportunity, these people will become intrigued with the prospect of delivering discretionary effort, but they will not know how to make it happen. They've got the latent talent... but the talent is *latent*. They're willing... but they don't know how to do more at work and still have a life apart from work.

It is your job to show these people how to make it happen, give them accountabilities that assume they will use their latent talent, and show them how to have a life apart from work. Put simply, it is your job to be a *Magnetic Leader*.

How Can You Do It All?

You can't.

Your body doesn't have a battery with unlimited capacity, your brain doesn't have boundless RAM, your emotions don't have built-in shock absorbers, and your vision doesn't look around corners. With this in mind, how can you lead and still take care of yourself? If you don't take care of yourself, how can you lead?

In a nutshell, you are not a leader... you're a person who leads. The well-being-under-pressure of all people—including leaders—depends on other people and certain conditions. The question you must answer is, "Upon what or whom will I depend?"

You depend on those who work for you. This is more difficult than it is obvious. To depend on those who work for you implies that you put your career in the hands of your employees, delegate sooner rather than later, accept their solutions even if they are not the solutions you would have chosen, and go home at night.

Secondly, you must depend on the future being unpredictable. This should be a little easier to do given the "Dot Bomb" crash, the Enron debacle, and the 9/11 abomination. But, in fact, each of us persists in our fantasy that "we will get things under control." The truth is you are not in control of your life any more than a surfer is in control of the wave.

How would you live differently if you truly believed your future was unpredictable? What alliances would you build? What skills would you refine? How would you spend your leisure time? How would you "stay on track" if you could not see the road ahead of you?

What Are The Chances You Will Succeed As A Leader?

It's not a matter of chance… it's a matter of courage, discipline, and humility.

First, let's define "leadership success." If leadership success means keeping your job, getting an annual cost of living increase and an occasional merit increase, and then retiring with a pension (i.e., "making your twenty"), then success is a matter of chance. If leadership success means attracting the best performing people to do the most challenging work under adverse conditions (i.e., *Magnetic Leadership*), then success is within your grasp.

"Making your twenty" worked into the early 90's, but it's a crapshoot today. Leaders whose strategy is to stay-off-everybody's-radar screen have thrown themselves into the rudderless and leaking life raft of the ordinary, the familiar, and the mediocre. Their future is grim because the emerging commercial world is extraordinary, unfamiliar, and unpredictable. What business plan included the meteoric rise of dot.coms… or their Icarus-like plummet? Which bomb detection companies were ready for the rocketing demand on 9/12/01? Can any company be prepared for the labor, production, distribution, legal, marketing, and financial consequences emanating from genetically engineered apples, cattle, water, and babies?

On the other hand, "leadership success" is within your grasp if success is defined by your ability to draw extraordinary performance out of ordinary people on a bumpy playing field shrouded in fog. Success is within your grasp because you are the competitive variable. Enterprises that succeed are, and will be, those that attract people who are ingenious, cooperative, resilient, bold, healthy, personable under pressure, and more than willing to walk into the unknown... employees who are determined to deliver discretionary effort. If you are a leader whose business objectives are unattainable apart from discretionary effort, who rewards discretionary effort, removes anything that stands in the way of that effort, and who is as dedicated to the prosperity of your people as you are dedicated to your own prosperity, then you will attract that kind of employee.

If you are that kind of leader, if you are a *Magnetic Leader*, then you are a rare breed... and you are in very high demand. You are a rare breed because most people in today's leadership positions have gotten there by excelling at leadership principles that worked in a stable and predictable world. They don't know how, and they don't want to learn how, to lead in the emerging world of global work.

All that stands in your way is you... and that is a formidable obstacle.

Do you have the courage to lead in a way you have not seen?

Be careful.

Leading as a magnet means you upset those employees who have carved out comfortable niches in the world of winning-is-getting-more-than-you-give. You will awaken the sleeping giants among leaders who want to retire before the performance bar is raised. Taking this "tack" means "taking your hands off the tiller" more often than not. Do you have the courage?

Do you have the discipline to lead in a way you have not seen? Do you have the discipline to stick with data-driven decisions... especially when you are swamped with crises and undercut by short staffing? Do you have the discipline to invest more in your best performing people even though their "wheels" don't "squeak"? Do you have the discipline to rest your team regularly even though the deadline is so close you can smell it? Do you have the discipline to return your team's attention to their proud history even though the future is filled with nothing but bad news? Do you have the discipline to go home and grow your life-apart-from-work even though the game-at-work will be won or lost within the next two weeks? Do you have the discipline?

The uncharted seas of the emerging world of work are too vast for any single leader to comprehend… and the anxiety of not knowing is more than a person can bear. Do you have the humility to admit that you need help to be a *Magnetic Leader*?

Ultimately your success depends on your willingness to wisely and specifically trust others. Obviously, you must trust those who work for you. Not so obviously, you must trust others… others who can lead *you*. It is this second group which you must trust with your vision of yourself as a leader, your fears and your vulnerabilities as a leader, your willingness to hear them as they attempt to draw the best out of you. You must give these few people permission to be your *Magnetic Leaders*.

Will you lead?

Vic Downing

I have listened for 25 years.

I have listened to leaders. When their careers were winding down they talked about mentors, nemeses, triumphs, and the genesis of each. First-time leaders, whose optimism was boundless and fears were barely suppressed, spoke of the irresistible gravitational pull of the possible. Leaders who were being crushed by circumstances or suffocated by their own poor decisions and lack of discipline had alot to say about what derails a leadership career and what revives a career-on-the-rocks.

I have listened to business owners. They led me into the frontiers of commerce... an uncharted territory of opportunity and danger. With passion and great respect they talked of the emerging customer, the new customer, the global customer. They showed me artifacts from the future... the new currency of absolute reliability, personable encounters, anticipatory innovation, and time compression. Every conversation ended with the same musing: "Where can I find people who are willing and capable of doing that kind of work?"

I have listened to the academicians who have built theories and models of what should work in the land of leadership. The more realistic of these agree that leadership is necessary, rarely executed, and always irresistible when it is executed.

I have listened to myself. I listened to my deep regrets and anger as an employee[4] who invested my best efforts and several years of my life following leaders who were more corrupt than talented... and who were exceptionally talented. On the other end of the spectrum, I listened to my admiration of two or three leaders who drew the best out of me like powerful magnets pulling metal fragments out of the sand. As a consultant[5] to national and global corporations in North America, Asia, and Europe, I listened to the think tank in my head as it wrestled with my clients' challenging assignments... every one of which was unachievable apart from the more-than-you-paid-for work of employees performing

---

[4] From 1985-1995 I worked for national and global companies. As an employee, I served as an individual contributor and as an executive.

[5] I started my consulting practice in 1976. My clients have included software, retail food, retail apparel, mixed technology, biotechnology, office products, manufacturing, universities, health care systems, The People's Republic of China, financial services corporations, pharmaceutical distribution, global intermodal transportation, and others. In those organizations I served executive leadership teams, customer service teams, sales teams, cross-functional teams, global teams, marketing teams, construction organizations, manufacturing groups, human resource departments, scientists, engineers, CEOs, CFOs, CIOs, and others.

under very adverse conditions.

Mostly I have listened to people who are not leaders and who daily decide between being people who cash paychecks or being people who deliver the kind of discretionary effort that makes the risk and expense of leadership worth it. They told me their desire to do more... and the disappointment they suffer at the hands of ordinary bosses. They described the thrill of doing more than they thought they could do... and how their leaders made that possible.

These people have a simple and clear message: please lead!

Bibliography

Pine II, B. Joseph and Gilmore, James H. <u>The Experience Economy</u>. Boston, Massachusetts: Harvard Business School Press, 1999.